J 956.94 HUG   GC
HUGHES, CHRIS
ISRAEL, NATIONS IN CONFLICT

GO  RY

D0564396

NATIONS IN CONFLICT

ISRAEL

by CHRIS HUGHES

**BLACKBIRCH®
PRESS**

San Diego • Detroit • New York • San Francisco • Cleveland • New Haven, Conn. • Waterville, Maine • London • Munich

© 2003 by Blackbirch Press™. Blackbirch Press™ is an imprint of The Gale Group, Inc., a division of Thomson Learning, Inc.

Blackbirch Press™ and Thomson Learning™ are trademarks used herein under license.

For more information, contact
The Gale Group, Inc.
27500 Drake Rd.
Farmington Hills, MI 48331-3535
Or you can visit our Internet site at http://www.gale.com

ALL RIGHTS RESERVED
No part of this work covered by the copyright hereon may be reproduced or used in any form or by any means—graphic, electronic, or mechanical, including photocopying, recording, taping, Web distribution or information storage retrieval systems—without the written permission of the publisher.

Every effort has been made to trace the owners of copyrighted material.

Photo credits: cover, pages 6, 10, 13, 14, 16, 17, 19, 23, 24, 27, 28-29, 36, 39, 41, 43 © CORBIS; page 5 (map) © Amy Stirnkorb Design; pages 6, 9 (inset), 11 © Corel Corporation; pages 20, 22 © AP Wide World; pages 34, 37 © Getty Images

LIBRARY OF CONGRESS CATALOGING-IN-PUBLICATION DATA

Hughes, Christopher (Christopher A.), 1968-
  Israel / by Chris Hughes.
     p. cm. — (Nations in conflict)
  Summary: Discusses the history, people, places, and future of the nation of Israel, where danger and conflict have always existed.
  Includes bibliographical references and index.
   ISBN 1-56711-525-X (hardback : alk. paper)
   1. Israel—Juvenile literature. [1. Israel.] I. Title. II. Series.

DS118 .H915 2003
956.94—dc21   2002014673

CONTENTS

A Holy Place

The country called Israel has had many names throughout history, including Canaan, Judah, Zion, and Palestine. It has also been called "the Holy Land," and for good reason: Israel and its city of Jerusalem are a central part of the history of three of the world's major religions. For Jewish people, Israel is the land that God promised to Moses, and the only land the Jews ever ruled completely. For Christians, it is the place where Jesus was born, lived, and died, and it contains all of Christianity's holiest sites. For Muslims, Israel is the place that holds one of the most sacred sites from Islam's history.

Israel has experienced a great deal of warfare and conflict through the centuries. Christians, Jews, and Muslims have all fought to control the region. Today, Israel continues to witness some of the worst violence in the world. There is little sign that the conflict will soon get better. At different times, the fighting has taken the form of declared wars, undeclared wars, and most often, terrorism—the illegal use of violence against a government or group of people by those who hope to achieve their own goals. Terrorism most often involves attacks on innocent civilians, and it has become a daily threat in Israel.

The current conflict is essentially a struggle between two groups: the citizens of Israel, who are mostly Jewish, and the mostly Muslim

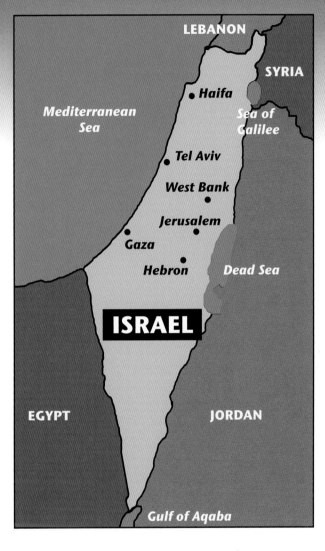

Palestinians who live within the borders of Israel but are not usually Israeli citizens. Many other nations have been involved in the dispute, including the United States and the countries that surround Israel. This outside involvement has caused the violence of the region to spread. The September 11, 2001, terrorist attacks against the United States can, in part, be linked to the fighting in Israel, as can many other terror attacks worldwide.

Much time and energy has been spent to try to bring peace to Israel. Although there have been brief periods without violence, the deep-rooted historic and religious claims to the land have defeated every attempt to stop the fighting permanently. The quest for long-term peace goes on.

CHAPTER ONE

Place, People, Past

Israel is part of the Middle East, which is the common name for the southwestern region of Asia. The Mediterranean Sea forms Israel's western border; Egypt lies to the south; and Jordan, Syria, and Lebanon are located to the east and north. Jerusalem is Israel's capital and most populated city. It is also home to some of the holiest sites for all three of the area's major religions—Judaism, Christianity, and Islam.

Israel is a small country, with slightly less area than the state of New Jersey. It has about 6 million people—fewer residents than New York City has. Almost 5 million Israeli citizens are Jewish; most of the rest are Arabs. (Arabs are people from the Middle East whose main language is Arabic.) Most Arabs are Muslim, though some are Christian and a fraction are Jewish. The countries that border Israel all have populations made up mainly of Muslim Arabs.

Israel has both fertile regions and barren desert. In the north, the land is wet and covered by hills and mountains. Northern and coastal Israel, where most of Israel's good farmland is found, are part of an area known as the Fertile Crescent. Some of the world's earliest farming began there. The rest of Israel is generally dry; the Negev Desert is

Jerusalem (pictured) is the capital of Israel.

located in the south. Israel's Dead Sea, found along the eastern border, is the lowest point on the earth's surface. The Jordan River runs from the north to the Dead Sea. Israel's weather is usually moderate, though some regions can become quite hot in the summer. Winter is wet in most areas except the southern-most desert.

Israel is much more industrialized than the nations around it. It produces many high-technology goods and services, and most of its people live in or near cities. Even though relatively few people work in agriculture, and much of the land is not suitable for farming, Israel is able to produce much of its own food because Israeli agriculture is quite advanced. The national economy is significantly stronger and the average income of Israeli citizens higher than in most other Middle Eastern nations.

Israel's Early History

Israel's history is well known to many people throughout the world: Christianity and Islam are the world's two largest religions, and both came from the foundation and traditions of Judaism. All three faiths trace their origins to common figures, including Adam, Abraham, Moses, and David.

The three religions all accept the story that Moses led the Jews out of Egypt, where they had lived in slavery, and brought them to Israel, the land they believed God had promised them. The Jews established a kingdom in Israel during the reigns of

The Dead Sea, located along Israel's eastern border, is the lowest point on earth.

הנקודה הנמוכה ביותר בעולם
394 מתר מתחת לפני ה ם
أوطأ نقطه في العالم ٣٩٤ مترتحت سطح البحر
THE LOWEST POINT ON
EARTH 394 M BELOW SEA
LEVEL

Ercole de' Roberti's painting, *Destruction of Jerusalem*, depicts the Roman invasion of Jerusalem in A.D. 70.

three consecutive kings: Saul, David, and Solomon. David captured Jerusalem and made it his capital, and his son, Solomon, built a holy temple there. After Solomon's rule, Israel fell into disorder and conflict. It was divided into two lands, and eventually, both were invaded and conquered by the Assyrians and Babylonians.

The Assyrians and Babylonians saw the Jews as a threat. They were afraid that if the Jews were allowed to remain in Israel, they would rise up and take back their "promised land." For that reason, these ancient empires scattered the Jews and made them live outside of Israel. The

Babylonians sacked Jerusalem and destroyed Solomon's temple.

In the first century B.C., the Roman Empire took over the region of Israel, which the Romans called Judea or Palestine. For many years, Jews fought unsuccessfully against Roman control. Finally, Rome passed laws that did not allow Jews to live in Israel. The most severe of these laws, passed in A.D. 135, forced the Jews out of Israel. They found new homes in Africa, Europe, or other parts of the Middle East.

Struggles for Control

Meanwhile, Israel continued to change hands. In the fourth century A.D., the Roman Empire became Christian and was divided; the eastern section, called the Byzantine Empire, kept control over the Middle East. Then, around 610, the religion of Islam was born. Muslims believe that the prophet Muhammad, who lived in what is now Saudi Arabia, received a visit from the Archangel Gabriel, and became a messenger of God (Allah). Muslims began to spread their faith throughout the region, and shortly after Muhammad's death in 632, the Muslims conquered Israel.

Beginning around 1096, European Christians fought a series of wars, called the Crusades, against the Muslims for control of Israel. The Christians wanted to regain the land where Jesus had lived and died. To Muslims, Jerusalem is holy because they believe the Archangel Gabriel brought Muhammad there one night, and that

The Dome of the Rock in Jerusalem is one of Islam's holiest sites.

Muhammad ascended to heaven from there. This journey is marked by Jerusalem's Dome of the Rock, one of Islam's holiest sites.

By 1300, the Muslims had defeated the last of the Christian forces, and life in Israel was fairly peaceful. Israel was occupied mainly by Arab Muslims, with very small Jewish and Christian populations. In the 1500s, the area was taken over by the Ottoman Empire. The Ottomans were Muslims from what is now Turkey. They let most of the Arab leaders of Israel continue to rule, as long as they paid Ottoman taxes. Jewish families who lived within the Ottoman Empire were usually treated well. They were allowed to practice their religion and follow their own leaders, as long as they paid taxes and did not disrupt society.

Most Jews, however, lived outside of Israel. Unlike those in Ottoman lands, the Jews who lived in Europe were often persecuted. They were not trusted by European Christians. Many Christians claimed that Jews had caused the death of Jesus, and Jews were often forced to live in ghettos. In most of Europe, Jews were not allowed to own land or hold political office. Banking was one of the few fields in which they were permitted to work, but as some Jewish bankers became wealthy, their success only created more resentment.

The Jewish Dream of a Homeland

As the years passed, European Jews began to dream of a land where they might be free from persecution. They believed that God had promised them Israel, and it was the only land Jews had ever ruled. By the end of the 1800s, Jews from Europe and the United States were trying to buy land in Israel. That land was still part of the Ottoman Empire, but it was populated mainly by Arabs who owned almost all of the good farmland. The only land available to the Zionists—people who supported the movement to return Jews to Israel—was in the desert. Over time, groups of Jews

Groups of Jews set up collective farms called kibbutzim in Israel to turn desert land into farmland.

began to move there. At first, few people in Israel protested. The Muslims owned so much land that the Jews were not seen as a threat. Although the effort to turn the desert into decent farmland was difficult, very slowly, the Jewish settlements grew. These settlements were collective farms called kibbutzim, where everyone shared in the work and the profits. As more Jews came to the region, Arab concerns began to mount.

World War I and English Rule

In 1914, World War I began. The Ottoman Empire, Germany, and others fought against England, France, and eventually, the United States. England found a way to use Israel to hurt the Ottomans. In two separate, vaguely written documents, England seemed to promise Palestine as an independent homeland to both the Jews and the Arabs if they agreed to oppose the Ottomans. When the war ended, it turned out that England and France had secretly agreed to split the Ottoman lands in the Middle East if they won. After they divided the lands, England took control of Israel.

The Arabs and the Jews both thought they deserved the land. Both groups believed they had historical and religious claims to it, and both argued that England had promised the land to them. For the next 30 years, the Arabs and the growing Jewish population fought against each other and against the English. This fighting was extremely violent and often unpredictable. Neither the Jews nor the Arabs were strong enough to fight directly against the well-armed and well-trained English soldiers. Instead, both sides used bombings, ambushes, and other terrorist tactics.

To decrease the tension and violence, the English tried to limit the number of Jewish people who entered Israel. Still, Jews continued to arrive, both legally and illegally. Although Jews made up just 10 percent of the population in 1920, that percentage had nearly tripled by 1939. Most of the Jews who came were young, strong, and prepared to fight for their homeland.

British forces arrived in Jerusalem in December 1917. England took control of Israel at the end of World War I.

THE DREYFUS AFFAIR AND EARLY ZIONISM

When the Romans expelled the Jews from Israel after A.D. 135, Jews scattered throughout the Middle East, Africa, and Europe. The Torah (the Jewish religious text) promised that the Jews would eventually regain Israel, so the idea of Israel, or Zion, became an image of both past and future security to many Jews. By the late nineteenth century, however, many Jews were tired of waiting.

A series of pogroms, or anti-Jewish riots, broke out in Russia and Poland in the 1870s and 1880s. Thousands of Jews were killed and many more were injured and left homeless. In Western Europe, life appeared to be better for Jews, at least until 1894. That year, a French military officer named Alfred Dreyfus was accused of selling military secrets to Germany. Part of the accusation was based on the fact that Dreyfus was Jewish and many Jews lived in Germany. The trial was held in

Alfred Dreyfus, here with his wife and children, was accused of selling military secrets to Germany.

secret, and Dreyfus never saw the so-called evidence against him. Dreyfus was convicted and sentenced to life imprisonment, and France erupted in anti-Jewish rallies and demonstrations. After

Crowds waited for a verdict outside the courtroom where Alfred Dreyfus was tried for espionage.

Dreyfus had spent five years in prison, the French admitted that he was innocent and released him.

Theodor Herzl was an Austrian journalist who was in France during the Dreyfus Affair. Herzl, also a Jew, believed that if Jews were to be mistreated throughout Europe, there was only one place where the Jewish people could expect to be safe. He wrote a book called *The Jewish State*, and helped create the World Zionist Organization in 1897. This group's goal was to establish a Jewish homeland in Palestine. Members began to raise money and to buy any available land in Israel. Soon, groups of Jews were sent to live on the newly bought land.

Some religious Jews protested this Zionist movement. They believed that, since God had promised to return the Jews to Israel, the Jews should not try to make that happen on their own. To Herzl and other early Zionists, though, the dangers for Jews in Europe were too great to allow them to wait any longer.

The Partition Plan

During World War II (1939–1945), millions of European Jews were imprisoned and killed in what is known as the Holocaust. Before, during, and after the war, many Jews fled Europe. Some of those who escaped slipped into Israel. When the war ended and the world learned about the Holocaust, there was great sympathy for the Jews. Many countries believed that the Jews should be allowed to establish their own country. Israel seemed to be the logical place because of its history, the number of Jews who already lived there, and the English promise from World War I. To the Arabs who made up more than two-thirds of Israel's population, this proposal did not seem fair at all.

England decided to turn the question over to the newly formed United Nations (UN). In August 1947, the UN voted to split the land into two parts. Areas that had a Jewish majority would become the state of Israel. Regions with an Arab majority would become Palestine. The cities of Jerusalem and Bethlehem, as well as some other places that were important to several groups, would become international areas controlled by the UN.

Although there were far more Arabs in the region than Jews, the UN gave more than half of the land to Israel. The plan for the new countries made the region look like a checkerboard: Israel would be made up of the northeast, much of the western coast, and the southeast, most of which was the Negev Desert. Palestine would include the southwest, the eastern area around Jerusalem and along the Jordan River, and the northwest.

To the Jews, the partition was not ideal, but without it, they had no claim to the area beyond the private lands the Zionists had bought. The plan gave the Jews an independent state, even if it was not as large as they had hoped and did not include Jerusalem. The Jewish leaders agreed

In the 1940s, many Jews fled Europe and arrived in Israel, where they went on to either kibbutzim or refugee camps.

to the plan. The Arabs, however, rejected it. They felt that the plan punished them in place of the Europeans who had mistreated the Jews during the war. They also did not believe that they, as the majority, should have to give up any land at all. They wanted complete independence both from England and the UN.

Although Arab leaders probably would not have agreed to any division of the land, they thought the UN partition was especially unfair. Most of the Arab and Muslim nations of the Middle East agreed. If the partition went into effect, they warned, the Arab states would not allow Israel to exist. Despite this threat, the UN went ahead with its plan.

CHAPTER TWO

Political Turmoil

On May 14, 1948, the English officially withdrew, and Israel declared itself an independent nation. This event had very different meanings to different groups of people. For the English, Israel's independence meant that they could finally end their unpopular rule. For the Arabs, it meant they would have to fight if they wanted to retake the land they believed was theirs. For the Jews, it brought both great celebration and fear for the future. Menachem Begin, a Jewish militant and a future prime minister of Israel, said, "It has been difficult to create our state. But it will be still more difficult to keep it going. We are surrounded by enemies who long for our destruction."[1]

The Middle East at War

The very next day, Egypt, Jordan, Syria, Lebanon, and Iraq all declared war on Israel. Although these nations had more soldiers than Israel (and most had air forces, which Israel lacked), the Israelis were better organized. They had taken advantage of the nine months since the partition decision to train soldiers, prepare leaders, and stockpile weapons that had been left behind by the English. The Palestinian Arabs, on the other hand, were

---

An explosion ripped through Jerusalem's Jewish business district in February 1948. The UN partition plan led to violence between Jews and Palestinians.

Refugees hiked from Palestine to Lebanon to escape the Arab-Israeli war.

disorganized. They lacked any strong central leadership, and looked instead to the surrounding nations for support.

Israel received a great deal of help from other nations, including political backing, money, weapons, and military training. When the fighting started, the Israelis were able to push back their Arab neighbors and win many key battles. By the time a cease-fire was declared in 1949, Israel had captured about half the land that had been set aside as Palestine. Three-quarters of a million Palestinians fled as refugees to nearby countries. The Arabs retained only the region around Jerusalem along the Jordan River and the Gaza Strip between Egypt and Israel, along the Mediterranean Sea. These two areas were taken over by Jordan and Egypt.

Israel quickly established political systems and built a military, with a great deal of international help. The United States was one of Israel's first and strongest supporters. U.S. weapons and training helped make Israel's army one of the best in the Middle East; Israel also received help from the Soviet Union, Czechoslovakia, England, and other nations with large Jewish populations.

Further Military Conflicts

Even after the 1949 cease-fire, tensions around Israel remained quite high. No Arab nation recognized Israel or had diplomatic relations with it, so there could be no peace treaties. There were some skirmishes in the 1950s; the largest was in 1956, when Israeli troops briefly occupied Egypt's Suez Canal. Then, in 1967, Israelis became convinced that they were about to be attacked by their neighbors. Instead, Israel launched a surprise attack on Egypt, Syria, and Jordan. In just six days, Israel defeated

Egypt and Syria attacked Israel in the 1973 October War.

all three nations' militaries. The Israelis took the Gaza Strip from Egypt and the west side (called the West Bank) of the Jordan River from Jordan. These lands became known as the Occupied Territories. Israel also captured the Golan Heights, an area in Israel's northeast, from Syria. Israel then controlled all the land that the UN had given to the Palestinians in 1947. The UN passed a resolution that called for peace and told Israel to withdraw from the new territory. Israel ignored it.

In October 1973, Egypt and Syria attacked Israel. Although the Arab armies were successful at first, Israel quickly recovered. By the end of the so-called "October War," Israel had protected all its territory and even invaded Egypt. These wars were not the only conflicts that involved Israel, however. Terrorism, which had been carried out regularly in the region since the English occupation after World War I, had become more frequent and more deadly.

The Palestine Liberation Organization

Each war had created more Palestinian refugees, and although some still lived within Israel, many more lived in the Occupied Territories of the Gaza Strip and the West Bank. Even more lived in Jordan and other nations. Small groups of Palestinians and other Arabs formed terrorist organizations. Their intention was to force Israel to give up its claim to the land. They used bombs

In 1969, Yasser Arafat became leader of the Palestine Liberation Organization.

and other weapons, often supplied by neighboring Middle Eastern nations, to attack Israeli military and civilian targets alike. In 1964, some of these groups came together under the leadership of the Palestine Liberation Organization, or PLO. In 1969, Yasser Arafat, leader of the terrorist al-Fatah group, became the PLO's leader.

The PLO charter, which defined the group's purpose, declared, "Armed struggle is the only way to liberate Palestine." The document also stated that there could be no compromise that would involve sharing the land, and demanded that Palestinians "reject all solutions which are substitutes for the total liberation of Palestine."[2] In other words, only the complete removal of the state of Israel would be acceptable.

The PLO kept up its terrorist attacks even when other nations began to change their relationship with Israel. In 1970, Jordan expelled Arafat, and he eventually moved PLO headquarters to Lebanon. In 1979, Egypt became the first Arab nation to sign a formal peace treaty with Israel. Despite this development, the PLO still continued to attack Israel. The Israelis, in turn, assaulted Palestinian targets, and at times, severely limited the rights of Palestinians who lived in Israel and the Occupied Territories.

Terrorism and Treaties

In 1982, in response to increased attacks by the PLO, Israel invaded Lebanon. There, Lebanese Christians who were allies of Israel entered two Palestinian refugee camps and massacred the people inside. Israeli forces remained in southern Lebanon until 2000. Because of this invasion, a new terrorist group called Hizballah was formed. The group's declared goals were to remove the Israelis from Lebanon and to destroy Israel entirely. Two other terrorist groups, Hamas and Islamic Jihad, also became active in the 1980s.

CAMP DAVID PEACE ACCORDS

In 1977, Egyptian president Anwar al-Sadat made a shocking and historic decision. He declared that he would travel to Israel to meet with the Israeli Knesset, or parliament, to discuss peace. Up to that point, no Arab leader had been willing to meet with any Jewish leader, much less actually travel inside Israel. In fact, no Arab nation, including Egypt, even recognized Israel's right to exist. Sadat himself had helped launch the October War against Israel in 1973.

By 1977, however, Sadat was secure enough as the leader of Egypt that he decided to take a significant political risk. By going to Israel, he hoped to work out a peace agreement that would return the Sinai Peninsula to Egypt. As he made his trip, he was well aware that the other Arab states of the Middle East and many of his own people did not approve of his

action. Still, Sadat believed that the possibility of peace was worth the loss of his popularity.

In Jerusalem, Sadat told the Knesset that he was ready to make peace with Israel. U.S. president Jimmy Carter had hoped for some time to find an opportunity to promote peace in Israel. He immediately invited Sadat and Israeli prime minister Menachem Begin to Camp David, the presidential retreat in Maryland. There, in 1978, Sadat and Begin worked out the Camp David Accords, which led to the Egypt-Israeli peace treaty, signed in 1979. Israel agreed to return the Sinai, and Egypt agreed to recognize Israel's right to exist. It was Israel's first peace treaty with an Arab nation, and the last one until it signed a treaty with Jordan in 1994.

For their efforts, both Sadat and Begin were awarded the Nobel Peace Prize in 1978. Sadat, however,

In 1979, Egyptian president Anwar Sadat (left), American president Jimmy Carter (center), and Israeli prime minister Menachem Begin (right) signed the Egypt-Israeli peace treaty.

paid a high price for his courageous decision. Egypt was expelled from the Arab League by the other Arab nations of the Middle East, and in 1981, Sadat was assassinated.

Even as these organizations grew, most Middle Eastern nations began to accept Israel. Jordan signed a peace treaty with Israel in 1994. Although Jordan and Egypt are still the only two Middle Eastern nations that have treaties with Israel, most other countries have moved toward more peaceful relations. Even Syria and Iran, nations often accused of funding terrorism, appear to have de-creased that aid in recent years. Syria and Israel have met to discuss the possible return of the Golan Heights taken by Israel in 1967.

Young Palestinians publicly opposed Israel's occupation of the Gaza Strip by throwing rocks at Israeli soldiers.

The Intifada

Even as the surrounding nations moved toward peace with Israel, internal conflicts remained. In 1987, a mass protest called the Intifada began in the Occupied Territories. Most of the protesters were young Palestinians. Often unarmed or armed with stones, they publicly opposed Israel's occupation of the West Bank and the Gaza Strip and the poor treatment of Palestinians in those areas. The Israelis often responded violently. In several instances, Israeli troops shot and killed unarmed rioters. News programs throughout the world showed pictures of the riots and helped win sympathy for the Palestinian cause.

The Intifada also highlighted the differences in how people lived in Israeli society. Then and now, the quality of life in Israel is quite high compared with that in other Middle Eastern nations. There is religious freedom and freedom of speech, and health care and education are excellent. Israelis also enjoy fine cultural events. Some of Israel's symphonies and performing arts groups are among the best in the world. As the Intifada showed, however, life was very different for Palestinians. Most Palestinians had no rights within Israel, but were not citizens of any other nation, either. Israel's exceptional opportunities were not necessarily open to Palestinians, most of whom lived in poverty.

The Palestinian National Authority

The worldwide attention and support that the Palestinians received as a result of the Intifada eventually led to a change in relations between Israel and the PLO. In 1988, the PLO recognized Israel's right to exist, and it officially gave up terrorism as a way to achieve its goals. With strong support from the United States and other countries, the PLO and the Israeli government began to work on possible peace plans. Israel agreed to allow the PLO to form a Palestinian National Authority, which began to create a government, police force, and the other systems needed to run a country. By 1993, the Intifada was over. In 1994, Arafat won the Nobel Peace Prize, along with Israeli prime minister Yitzhak Rabin and foreign minister Shimon Peres.

Beginning in 1994, parts of the West Bank and the Gaza Strip were turned over to Palestinian control. Although this was a sign of real

---

Israeli prime minister Yitzhak Rabin was shoved into his car by security guards after he was shot in 1995. Rabin died from his wounds.

progress, many Israelis were not pleased. Some believed it was unacceptable to give Palestinians territory to create their own state. They thought the Palestinians had lost their chance for their own nation when they turned down the UN partition in 1948. Others feared that the Israeli government would give away too much land. Many Israelis who lived in the Occupied Territories or the Golan Heights refused to move. In 1995, a Jewish student who believed that Rabin had betrayed Israel when he offered land to the Palestinians assassinated the Israeli leader.

The Violence Continues

On the Palestinian side, despite the PLO's decision to recognize Israel, radical groups such as Hamas and Hizballah still demanded nothing less than complete control of Palestine. These groups became even more violent. Suicide bombings, in which terrorists killed themselves as they exploded bombs in public places, occurred fairly often. One of the most common terrorist tactics in the 1990s was to explode bombs on crowded buses. When the Israelis retaliated, they sometimes targeted Palestinian civilians. In 1994, for example, an Israeli citizen shot more than 200 Muslims and killed 29 as they worshipped in a mosque.

The peace process continued, but each instance of violence slowed it down. The negotiations were also delayed by changes in government. Although Yasser Arafat kept consistent control of the PLO and Palestinian National Authority, Israel's leaders had to face regular elections. If a majority of Israelis thought too many concessions might be made to the Palestinians, the prime minister's job was in danger. Each time a new prime minister was chosen, the peace process was delayed further.

In September 2000, a new cycle of violence, called the "Second Intifada," began, and threatened all the progress that had already been

Political leader Ariel Sharon (center) surrounded by bodyguards, visited al-Aqsa Mosque in Jerusalem in 2000.

made. One of Israel's most powerful political leaders, Ariel Sharon, visited the site of the al-Aqsa Mosque in Jerusalem. This mosque is the most sacred Muslim site outside of Saudi Arabia. As the minister of defense during Israel's invasion of Lebanon, Sharon had failed to stop the massacre of the Palestinian refugees. For this and for other acts committed in his long military career, Palestinians called him "the butcher." Palestinians saw his visit to the Islamic holy site as an insult, and they responded with a series of riots. The riots stopped the peace process, and in 2001, concerned Israelis who wanted a strong leader elected Sharon as prime minister. From that point on, violence in Israel has become almost a daily event.

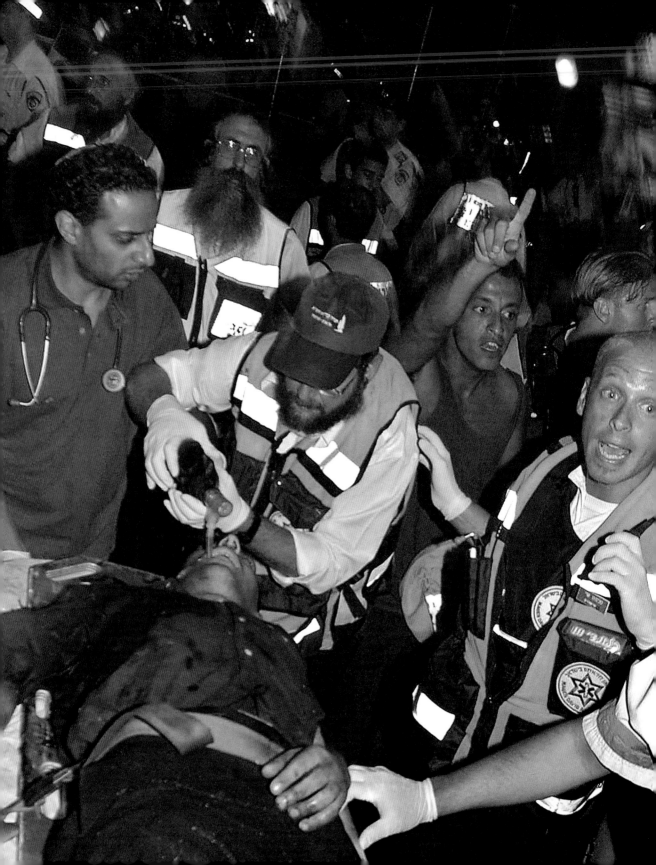

CHAPTER THREE

Israel's Future

Life in Israel has become more dangerous than ever for both Israelis and Palestinians. In the 20 months that followed the start of the Second Intifada, most sources estimated that more than 1,500 Palestinians and 600 Israelis were killed. Tens of thousands of others were wounded. Deaths caused by suicide bombings doubled in a one-year period. Suicide attacks occurred at weddings, universities, prayer services, and in crowded markets, among other places.

Daily Dangers

These violent acts have forced Israelis and Palestinians to think twice about the simplest daily events. Riding a bus, eating at a sidewalk café, and going to a synagogue or mosque can all be dangerous activities. People in Israel are less willing to go out when they do not have to, which means there are fewer cultural and social events. Terrorist attacks have further isolated Jews from Arabs. Before the Second Intifada began, nonmilitant Palestinians and Israelis often had social or business connections with each other. Many of those relationships have been damaged by mutual distrust and by Israeli regulations that have restricted the Palestinians' movement and ability to communicate.

Suicide bombings have killed many people in Israel.

Above: In response to suicide bombings, Israeli soldiers refused to let Palestinians leave the city of Ramallah.

Right: More than 1,500 Palestinians were killed during the first two years of the Second Intifada.

The Israeli response to terrorist attacks was widespread. Towns in the West Bank and Gaza were occupied by the Israeli military, and curfews— times during which people are not allowed outside their homes—were established. A curfew might be at night only, or it might cover most or all of the day for several days at a time. Travel between Palestinian areas and from Palestinian areas into Israel was severely limited. Israel's government

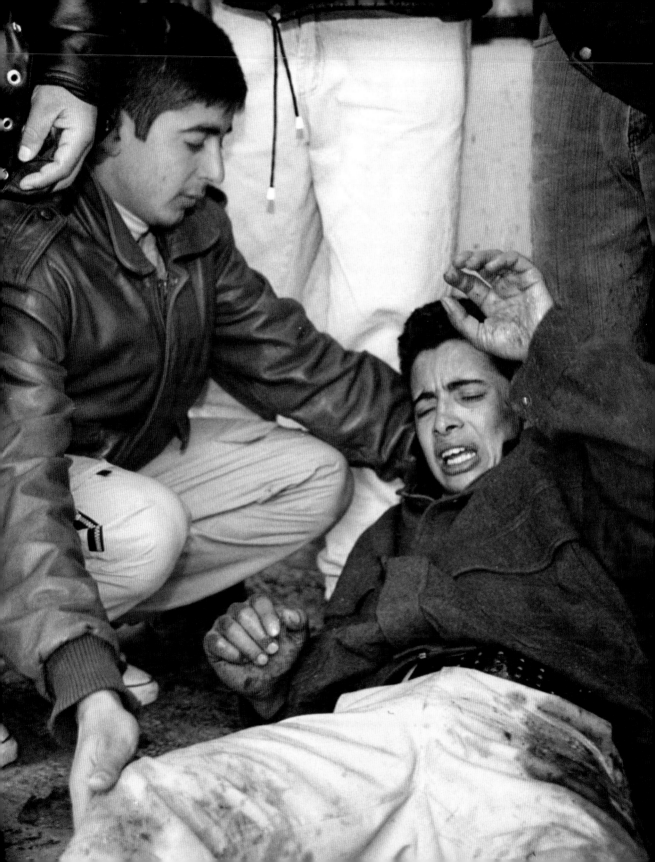

estimated that slightly more than 600 noncombatant, or nonfighting, Palestinians were killed in the first two years of the conflict; Palestinian estimates were higher. The travel limits and curfews had a huge impact on the Palestinian economy, as Palestinian businesses lost a great deal of money.

The Israelis did not punish the people alone. Individual Palestinian leaders were targeted in assassination attempts. Several leaders of Hamas were killed or captured, as were other leaders who were believed to have planned suicide attacks. Israeli tanks and bulldozers destroyed the homes of several suspected terrorists. Arafat himself was trapped in his home and office for weeks during the conflict. In 2002, Arafat declared, "We would like to establish peace in the region, not only for us but also for the Israeli people."[3] Still, Israeli leaders did not think he had done enough to stop the suicide attacks.

The Second Intifada has put the peace process almost completely on hold. Though both governments claim that they want to move ahead with plans to create a Palestinian state, Israelis and Palestinians seem to have lost faith that the two nations will be able to exist side by side. Fear and distrust has increased, and neither side seems willing to give in to the demands of the other.

Issues for Consideration

There are other obstacles to peace besides the ongoing violence. One concern is the same issue that faced the UN in 1948: there is a majority of Palestinians in two different regions—the Gaza Strip and the West Bank—but these places are separated by areas that have Jewish majorities. Unless the Jewish Israelis are removed, any Palestinian state will be partly divided by Israeli territory. Many Israelis have moved to traditional Palestinian lands even within the Occupied Territories, sometimes to increase Israel's

In October 2000, Israeli border policemen refused Palestinians entry to al-Aqsa Mosque.

claim to the region. Some of those people will refuse to move even if Palestine becomes a separate state.

Another major challenge to the peace process is the fear, distrust, and anger among people on both sides. Countless Israelis and Palestinians have had family members or friends killed or wounded in the conflict. Each side strongly believes that its own claim to the land is the valid one.

HAMAS: FIGHTING FOR PALESTINE

Hamas is a group established in 1987 in the Gaza Strip. The name is an acronym for Islamic Resistance Movement, though the word hamas also means "zeal" in Arabic. Several of the group's founders were members of the Muslim Brotherhood movement that was active in Egypt through the 1970s. Hamas appeared at about the same time that the first Palestinian Intifada started. Like the PLO, Hamas believes that Palestinians should have their own homeland of Palestine. Unlike the PLO, however, Hamas refuses to share the region with Israel. It does not recognize Israel's right to exist.

Led by Sheik Ahmad Yassin, Hamas has been responsible for most of the suicide bombings in Israel since 1993. This has put the group at odds with the PLO and Yasser Arafat, whom Israel has called upon to stop the terrorist attacks so that peace talks can move forward. Most Hamas leaders live and operate in secret, because both Israel and the Palestinian National Authority target them for capture or assassination.

Many Palestinian people, however, support Hamas. The organization is more than just a terrorist group. With money given to it by nations such as Iran and Syria, it has built and supported schools, health centers, orphanages, and mosques throughout the Gaza Strip and the West Bank. To some Palestinians, Hamas seems to do more to actively protect Palestinian interests than does Arafat's Palestinian National Authority. Despite the benefits the group has offered the people, though, the nature of its actions has brought the peace process to a standstill and placed both Palestinians and Israelis at greater risk than ever.

Members of Hamas protested the Israeli-Palestinian peace accord in 1993.

In fact, the same claims that Jews made in 1947—that they had no homeland, had faced years of persecution, and had a long history on the land—can all be made by Palestinians today. Groups on both sides who do not want to share the land feed fears as they launch attacks and continuously restart the violence.

The conflict has spread to the rest of the world as well. Both Israelis and Palestinians have been attacked in other countries, and nations that support either side have also been targeted. In particular, international terrorist organizations have criticized and attacked the United States for its longtime support of Israel. Terrorist groups such as al-Qaeda, which was responsible for the September 2001 attacks on the World Trade Center and Pentagon in the United States, have won many followers by speaking against U.S. support for Israel.

The Holy City of Jerusalem

Perhaps the single biggest factor that threatens the peace process is the status of Jerusalem. Israel and Palestine both see Jerusalem as their capital and as the most historically important city in the region. In the words of Elhanan Leib Lewinsky, a Jewish writer in the early twentieth century, "Without Jerusalem, the land of Israel is a body without a soul."[4] Any plans to divide Jerusalem and use it as a shared capital must consider the question of how to split the city. The Temple Mount, which includes Islam's al-Aqsa Mosque and Dome of the Rock, is believed to be the place where Abraham offered to sacrifice his son to God. It is also the site of the Western Wall. This wall is all that remains of the ancient Jewish temple built on the ruins of Solomon's temple before the Roman conquest. Neither the Israelis nor the Palestinians would accept a division if it kept them away from this holy area.

TERROR IS OUR COMMON ENEMY

Palestinians held a vigil in Jerusalem one day after the September 11, 2001, terrorist attacks on America.

Despite several meetings between Israeli and Palestinian leaders (almost always arranged with help from an outside nation), the cycle of violence has regularly stopped any real progress. Until both the Israelis and Palestinian leaders can control their own people, including groups that use terror as a weapon, Israel will remain a land in conflict. Hope for a peaceful future is tied to the willingness of both sides to put aside violence. If they can move past the years of war and dispute, there may yet be a bright future ahead.

Important Dates

1914–1918	World War I takes place.
1915	A series of letters between Arab leader Husayn Ibn-Ali (sharif of Mecca) and England's high commissioner Sir Henry McMahon appear to promise independence to Arabs, which Arabs believe includes Palestine.
1917	England's foreign secretary Lord Balfour issues declaration that promises English support for "a national home for the Jewish people" in Palestine.
1922	England receives mandate over Palestine.
1939–1945	World War II takes place.
1947	UN recommends partition of Palestine.
1948	English mandate ends; Israel declares independence on May 14.
1948	First Arab-Israeli war begins on May 15.
1949	War ends; region assigned to Palestine taken over by Israel, Egypt, and Jordan.
1956	Israeli troops temporarily occupy Suez Canal in Egypt.
1964	Palestine Liberation Organization (PLO) formed.
1967	Israel invades Egypt, Syria, and Jordan in Six-Day War; takes over West Bank (including Jerusalem), Gaza Strip, and Golan Heights.

1969	Yasser Arafat becomes leader of PLO.
1970	PLO expelled from Jordan.
1973	Israel invaded by Syria and Egypt in October War (also called Yom Kippur War or Ramadan War).
1978	Israeli prime minister Menachem Begin and Egyptian president Anwar Sadat win Nobel Peace Prize for agreement to make peace.
1979	Egypt-Israeli peace treaty signed.
1982	Israel invades Lebanon to attack PLO posts; Palestinian civilians killed in Sabra and Shatilla refugee camps.
1987	First Intifada begins, which draws world attention to the Palestinian cause.
1988	Yasser Arafat recognizes Israel's right to exist and renounces terrorism for PLO.
1993	First Intifada ends.
1994	Israel and Jordan sign peace treaty.
1994	Israeli-Palestinian agreement signed; Yitzhak Rabin and Shimon Peres (Israel) and Yasser Arafat (Palestine) win Nobel Peace Prize.
1995	Yitzhak Rabin assassinated.
2000	Ariel Sharon visits Temple Mount; Second Intifada begins.
2001	Sharon elected prime minister.

For More Information

WEBSITES

www.al-bab.com	Arab Gateway: website with information and links to Arab nations.
www.arab.net	News and information about Arab nations and Arab culture.
www.cfrterrorism.org	Website for Council on Foreign Relations (publisher of *Foreign Relations* magazine) with information on international terrorist groups.
www.idf.il	Official website for Israeli military (Israeli Defense Force).
www.ict.org	Website for the Institute for Counter-Terrorism: Israeli institute with information on the Arab-Israeli conflict and international terrorism.
www.mfa.gov	Official website of government of Israel (Ministry of Foreign Affairs) with news reports and links.
www.palestinercs.org	Website for Palestine Red Crescent Society: aid and relief organization within Palestine.
www.pna.gov.ps	Official website of Palestinian National Authority.
www.us-israel.org	Virtual Jewish Library: sections on history, religion, politics, and relations.

BOOKS

The Arab-Israeli Conflict, by Tony McAleavy (SIGS Books and Multimedia, 1998).

The Creation of Israel, Linda Jacobs Altman (Lucent Books, 1988).

Israel and the Arab World, by Heather Lehr Wagner (Chelsea House, 2002).

Yasser Arafat, by David Downing (Heinemann Library, 2002).

Yitzhak Rabin: Israel's Soldier Statesman, by Michael G. Kort (Millbrook Press, 1996).

Source Quotations

1. Quoted in William Safire, ed., *Lend Me Your Ears: Great Speeches in History* (New York: W.W. Norton, 1992), p. 66.

2. Helena Cobban, *The Palestinian Liberation Organization* (New York: Cambridge University Press, 1984), p. 43.

3. Quoted online at The Palestinian National Authority, www.pna.gov.ps; accessed August 2002.

4. Elhanan Leib Lewinsky, quoted on-line at "The Jewish Virtual Library," www.us-israel.org; accessed August 2002.

About the Author

Chris Hughes holds a B.A. in history from Lafayette College and an M.A. in social studies education from Lehigh University. A history teacher and school administrator, Hughes teaches both U.S. and world history and has written several books on the American Civil War and on developing nations. Hughes currently lives and works at a boarding school in Chatham, Virginia, with his wife, Farida, and their children, Jordan and Leah.

Index

GORDON COOPER BRANCH LIBRARY
Phone: 970-963-2889
76 South 4th Street
Carbondale, CO 81623